SLEEPING HABITS AND ROUTINES

SLEEP IN YOUR OWN BED

HUNI HUNFJORD

SLEEPING HABITS AND ROUTINES

SLEEP IN YOUR OWN BED

HUNI HUNFJORD

This book is a work of non-fiction.

For information contact:
Kirkjuvegur 28, 230 Keflavik, Iceland
phone: +354 821 1977
http://www.HuniHunfjord.com

Cover design by Huni Hunfjord
Book design, editing and formatting by Watchon Publishing

ISBN: 978-9935-9342-7-7
First Edition: April 2017

TABLE OF CONTENTS

HUNI HUNFJORD

SLEEPING ROUTINES

Watchon has gathered together the experiences of many great parents and experts to share with you and your family. Watchon teaches children and coaches parents to create a good family environment at a very early age.

Here are some of the reasons parents convince themselves that their child should be in their bed instead of their own bed:

- We see that the child feels more comfortable there.

- We feel it's easier to put the child to sleep there.

- We are still breastfeeding, so we need to have him/her close by!

- We love the child so much and it feels so great to have this little human cuddling with us.

- Why should we try to discipline this little poor thing? We will do that later in life when he/she understands more.

How would you feel, if you were told that by allowing your child to sleep in your bed, you are possibly setting yourself up for failure? You might be risking your relationship and you are creating a dependance which will be harder to overcome the longer you hang on to this routine of allowing your child to sleep in your bed. A routine is something you do more often than not. Are you allowing your child to sleep in your bed more often than not? It is very good for you and the child, to start at a very young age and have him or her sleep in their own bed, even from the first day home from the hospital, but you can always make an exception to the rule every now and then. For example if you fall asleep along with the child by accident, after playing with the child in your bed or if the child gets sick at a young age they need us more than ever and it's draining to take care of a sick child and therefore you might fall asleep together. You should nevertheless move the child to it's own bed as soon as you wake up and realize the child is in still in your bed with you. If you want your child to sleep as soundly a possible, from the first day home from the hospital, you should already have a crib waiting at home for the child. While the child is still breastfeeding, it is OK to have the crib in your room but under no circumstances should you be tempted to have the child sleep in your bed. At first it can be hard for many parents to put the child in their own bed (crib). Looking at your little child fast asleep, you (the parent) probably just want to hold your little angel as close to you as long as you can, and these feelings are perfectly normal. When a human being becomes a parent they produce a hormone called oxytocin, this hormone makes them fall in love with their baby, it creates a very strong bond. This is true for both parents, though in greater quantities with the mother. The mother will produce oxytocin and pass it through her breast feeding, creating a very powerful bond with the child. Later it will be even harder to turn things around without help if you start off on the wrong foot and have the child sleep in your bed. Don't worry if you are reading this with a child that needs some adjustments with her/his sleeping habits, this short booklet can help you.

If you are having trouble putting your child to bed today, regardless of what you did, or did not do, you can reverse the situation today. Let's get started!

With these easy steps to follow, we guarantee that you will be enjoying crying-free grownup evenings in 2-6 days from now if you follow each step very carefully.

STEP ONE – PREPARE

Preparing your child for a routine and setting boundaries. By doing that you are letting the child gain their own space as well and reclaiming yours. By teaching your child about boundaries you are also nurturing their independence and self-confidence.

No matter how old your child is, you need to prepare the child timely before he/she is supposed to go to sleep. This needs to be on a regular basis and as consistent as possible, because it creates the perfect automatic routine for the child. If you decide that the child should be a sleep at 8pm then you need to prepare the child approximately 30 minutes before or at 7.30pm. Talk to the child and say something that indicates what is about to happen, example: "We are getting ready for bed in 10 minutes" or say "its time to put on your pajamas." You decide what you will use to trigger this routine we are about to teach you how to create. This is something you try to have as constant as possible. Make sure that during the next 6-7 days you will have time to implement this change of routine every day. When we trigger a chain of events, we want it to become as automatic as possible. If you want to create a trigger point on you child, using the NLP approach (Neuro-linguistic programming), then decide what will be your trigger. You could for example take both of your hands and put them on top of each shoulder on your child and then tell your child with a smile "Go play now, after 10 minutes we are putting on our pajamas and brushing our teeth". The more you are pleased and excited about the process the more your children will be enthusiastic themselves. You may choose whatever trigger your desire, just make sure to be consistent in your execution, doing it over and over again, not changing it up, since that would defeats the purpose. This can be done verbally as well as physically and by touching the child in a certain way and speaking certain words at the same time you are combining two sensory factors to the trigger, making it even more powerful.

STEP TWO – PRE-GAME

The lead-in time is from the time you activate the trigger by telling your child what is about to happen. (see step one) until the time the child actually goes to bed. This part is like a pre-game ritual or like a professional basketball player shooting free throws. Have you ever seen how athletes do the same thing before each game or how a basketball player dribbles the ball exactly the same way each time before shooting a free throw? If you have then great, then you understand the importance of repetition. If you haven't, then take a look next time you see a basketball game on TV or ask someone you know, if they have any routines in their lives that they repeat over and over again until it becomes muscle memory. Muscle memory is something we do and don't have to think about it, we just do it, like walking for example. Muscle memory is doing something with your muscles, it is controlled by your subconscious mind once you have done it so many times you don't have to think about it any more, it becomes a reaction or an automatic response to a trigger. When we start to walk, for the first time, we need to concentrate on it until we have repeated it enough times that it becomes muscle memory. You and I, we can walk today and focus on something else, yet while we are walking, a million things are going on in our bodies without our attention, we blink our eyes, our heart beats, we fight bacteria, we digest food and so on. The great think about the subconscious mind is that we can train it to take over the most unlikely things things in life and become as automatic as our heartbeat.

From the moment you activate the trigger, you need to watch the time very carefully and maybe to be on the safe site, it would be best to be near the child during this time. If your child is playing in his/her room, then go play for 10 minutes with the child or watch a cartoon together with your child. Once the ten minutes have passed you need to lead your child to the bathroom and brush his/her teeth and if you usually do something else in the bathroom, like brushing the hair or whatever you have done in the past, just keep that in the routine as well. When the we are done brushing the teeth it is very important to ask her/him to try to use the potty while you are still in the bathroom and if your child is still wearing a diaper then this is a very good practice to take off the diaper and sit them for 2-3 minutes on the toilet, then put a fresh diaper one on right after that training session. You are forming a relationship between sitting on the toilet and getting a clean diaper after sitting on the toilet. Put a clean one on, even if you just changed the diaper a few minutes ago. This is to make sure it is in the ritual (lead-in time) you are setting up for you child. Now it's time to go to bed!

STEP THREE – GOODNIGHT

Now it should be very close to 8pm. You walk with your child or carry it, depending on its age, to it's bedroom. Here it is up to you, if you want to say a prayer or sing a song to the child or even tell a short story. In some cases you may just wish the child sweet dreams and a give a goodnight's kiss. When you are finished with the story/singing/teaching/kissing, you tell our child to lay down and you say "goodnight" and walk calmly away from the bed. You do this regardless whether the child is sleeping in their own room or even if the child is still sleeping in your room in it's own crib. You pause at the door and leave the door slightly open, almost shut. By leaving the door ajar you are giving the child some comfort knowing you are out there and it is easier for you to monitor their progress through the small opening of the door, instead of having to open the door and make noise. Turn of the lights before you leave the door ajar. Remember that it is OK for a child to cry. In many cases it is even unavoidable if you want to help them to learn to control their behavior. We are not born with self-control, that's why children need to learn that from the parents, this also applies to older children especially toddlers. It is useful to know that if you are implementing this process of creating a sleeping ritual at a later stage, rather than from day one. It is common for a child to cry if it is being taught new behaviors, like sleeping in it's own bed for example, or if it has been taking long hours putting your kid to bed in the past and now you are finally developing a 30 minute ritual. For very young children it can be a very good idea to put their blanket or cover firmly around the baby's body and yes of course we make sure to be very careful not wrapping the blanket around the face only tightly around the body. This gives the young child comfort. Bear in mind that it is not so long ago that the child was still in the womb and it felt very safe and secure there, by wrapping the blanket tightly around the baby's body, it often gets that same feeling of security. This usually only applies to very young children but in some cases older children like it as well, just give it a try.

STEP FOUR – SLEEPING BUDDY

Creating a perfect sleeping buddy might be a very nice add on to your process of creating a good sleeping ritual for your child.

If your child is less than 6 months old then you can skip this step if you like, but if you child is older than 6 months, then this approach might apply and it might benefit this process quite a bit. You will have to determine what is the best sleeping buddy your child can have. This can be anything the child loves the most. A teddy bear, favorite blanket, favorite pacifier or any other non-sharp object that the child likes to carry around with them all the time. Remember to avoid having anything in the bed with a child 6 months old or younger to prevent choking hazard.

STEP FIVE – STAY

Rule #1 at this stage, is to never take the child out of their bed unless injured, sick or having to use the bathroom.

When or if the child starts to call for you, or even cry, don't run directly into the room. After about one minute, call into the bedroom with a calm voice and tell them to go to sleep. If the child continues to cry or continues calling for you then you walk up to the door and look inside the room, try to avoid turning on the light in the room. Say "goodnight" and walk calmly away after you have made sure that there are no injuries nor is the child sick. The first evening in the process of creating a sleep ritual this might take some time, so be patient and keep it up and this will pay off big time for you and the child very soon. If your child keeps crying, you repeat the process over and over again, calmly answering them after a minute first time, waiting two minutes the second time, three minutes the third time and so on. And between rounds if the child is still crying the whole time, go to the bedroom door and look inside and tell the child to go to sleep. Each cycle with the same calm voice and patience. If this child starts to get worse and you are very concerned you can enter the room and go to the child, but remember rule#1 don't pick the child up, it might be enough to touch the hand or just your presence close to the child might do the trick. If the child calms down by you doing this, then you have verified that the child is not sick nor injured, it is simply wanting to control the situation and is facing fear since it's in an unknown situation for the child. We, as humans are wired to feel fear when we step into the unknown, when we step outside our comfort zone, this is hardwired into our DNA and that's exactly what is happening to your child, uncalled for fear creeping in as the child heads into the unknown. After a short period head back to the door and say good night and repeat the process. The child will eventually fall asleep and you must be very patient and consisted in our approach developing this new ritual, it will be worth it for the both of you. In my experience the first night is going to be the hardest and if you succeeded in following rule #1, then I promise that tomorrow will be much easier.

GAMES

Game to play in this process of creating sleeping habits and rituals.

It can be fun to create a game to make this process more exciting for you child, after the age of one years old. Get a digital clock so you can tell the time on in the dark. Hide the minutes (with tape for example) and when you put the child to bed point at the hours and say its 8 o'clock, time for bed, and tell the child that no one should be out of bed before 5 o'clock for example. Make this a fun thing for your child, you will be surprised how quickly they learn. By the time our child has learned the hours very well, then you can show the minutes on the clock.

REWARD SYSTEM

If your child is old enough to understand rewards by explaining it, then it can be a great game and motivation for the child to collect stars on a piece of paper you keep visible beside the bed each time the child goes to bed without fussing. You must then have the game set up so the child knows, for example, after reaching 10 stars there is a prize waiting for them. It should be something special you would normally not give them each day, and has to be worth winning.

POSSIBLE SCENARIOS

If the child wants a glass of water to drink for example, it is OK to get a glass of water and bring it to the child, but remember rule #1, don't take the child out of bed for that drink of water. If you can leave a little water in a plastic cup on the nightstand when you leave the room, with very little water in the glass, this is mostly for comfort. If your child is acting out, crying and trying different things, then it is and will continue to be creative to get your attention, trying to get you to reach in and pick the child up, don't fall for it. Short term sacrifice listening to a little crying, for a long term gain of having a solid sleep ritual where you child goes to bed without any fuss or trouble at all.

If the child become afraid of something, like a shadow, moving curtains or "monster" under the bed. Take a water spray bottle and mark it as monster poison and go into the room and take care of the problem, spray under the bed or closet. If it's the curtain, fix is so that it doesn't move. If it's any shadows from furniture just move the furniture around until the shadow disappears. Remember rule #1, the child should be in bed during this process. When finished walk to the door and repeat the same thing as before, almost closing the door and saying goodnight and walking calmly away. If your child does not calm down and is still afraid of the darkness in the room then it is OK to leave a small flash light by the bed, preferably skip this step if possible or have a small night lamp lid somewhere in the room.

If the child wets the bed. You will in this case have to remove the child temporarily, but only while you change the sheets, and then repeat the process from step three again.

If the child tells you that it is afraid of a noise (assuming the child is at the age of speaking of course) you should be able find what the cause is and take care of it. If you find out the noise is from yourself or the TV you are watching, then offer the child to close the door all the way shut, right before you leave the room. Usually the child will not want that at all and then you know it was not a real frightening situation but instead, just one more tactic the child was trying out to see if it was possible to gain control of the situation.

If you are dealing with an older sibling you might find yourself in the situation where the older sibling is being jealous of the younger one, which is still in the master bedroom in his/her crib or even worse sleeping in the master bed. Sometimes crying is the only way they know how to get more attention. This is something to deal with while awake, just make sure you pay attention to details if this might be the case when you are creating a sleeping ritual to an older sibling.

If the child sneaks into your bed during the night you should always return them calmly to their own bed as soon as you notice it. A large part of creating a ritual is for them to wake up in their own bed.

TO BEAR IN MIND

All children are individuals with different needs. You the parent need to add your personal touch on to this program. What it may be, is up to you. You don't need to add your own flavor to the process, but putting your personal touch on it, makes it so much more fun!

HABITS

The myth about doing something for 21 days to form a new habit for life has been overruled by science today, in fact it takes about 66 days to make new behavior into a lifelong habit. This varies of course between people, anywhere from 2 months to 9 months is the normal amount of time it takes to form a new habit for life. What about children? Children are much, much faster to develop new habits for life. One of the reasons is that they are currently developing habits, not changing their habits. A child can form a new habits for life by doing the same new behavior for 5 days in a row. But there is a weakness to this fast learning curve as well, it only takes about 5 days to undo a behavioral pattern as well. So in other words when you have success, after following these simple steps it is up to you to follow through and keep up the behavior next week, the week after that and so on.

That should be really easy once you have succeeded the first week with this process in this book.

Now you are ready to start the journey, it can be fun and rewarding or long a hard, that is totally up to you, what mindset are you going to adapt before you start the progress?

TIME FOR CHANGE IS NOW!

Watchon Indicator.

IN CLOSING

Dear reader, thank you for reading this book. This book was written 2 years before I finally published it. It has been my pleasure to share with you my experience and others that have sent me their story on how to transition their child from the master bed into their own. I hope you got some value from reading this and I want to tell you how much I appreciate you and being able to share this with you. Thank you, you are awesome!

Sincerely, the author,

Huni Hunfjord.

THE AUTHOR HUNI HUNFJORD

Huni Hunfjord is the author of *Sleeping Habits and Routines, Top 1% Parents Raise Top 1% Children, The Mentorian, Our Road without Boundaries* and Founder of the Watchon brand and Focus Gym ♡♡ Be you! As a father of three, children and entrepreneurship are core to his life. Huni loves creating apps, music videos, new ventures, coaching and creating interactive stories centered around children that parents can use to help them grow and develop into the best possible version of themselves. This book has been created for parents to create great sleeping habits and rituals with their children.

OTHER BOOKS BY HUNI HUNFJORD

Top 1% Parents Raise Top 1% Children

Our Road without Boundaries

The Mentorian

Læringinn

LEARN MORE ABOUT HUNI HUNFJORD

http://amazon.com/author/HuniHunfjord

http://HuniHunfjord.com

http://IcyDesign.com

Learn more about the Watchon Brand

http://Watchon.Club

Learn more about Focus Gym ♡ ♡ Be you!

http://FocusGymBeyou.com

ONE LAST THING...

If you enjoyed this short book I'd be very grateful if you'd post a short review on Amazon. Your support really does make a difference and I read all the reviews personally so I can get your feedback and make this book even better.

If you'd like to leave a review then all you need to do is review this book on its author's page on Amazon here:

http://amazon.com/author/HuniHunfjord

or,

if you have purchased a printed copy of the book, please send your review directly to testimonial@HuniHunfjord.com as we would love to include your review on our website.

Thanks again for your support!
Huni Hunfjord